ALPHABET SOUP

TO FEED ...

THE HOPEFUL MIND

Alphabet Soup to Feed the Hopeful Mind

Jana Baron and Lesia Zablockij

Publishing by 10-10-10 Publishing, Markham Ontario

Copyright 2021 by Jana Baron and Lesia Zablockij

No part of this publication can be reproduced, stored in a retrieval system or transmitted in any form or by any means, electronic, mechanical, photocopying, recording, scanning or otherwise.

All rights reserved, including the right to reproduce this book or portions thereof in any manner whatsoever.

ISBN:

Acknowledgement

This is a joint Acknowledgement from the authors. Life has its ups and downs. It's only when we bridge the fear, to really know who we are inside, that we can fully embrace all that we are meant to be.

The good and the bad provide us with lessons to improve our future. Coming face to face with the fear is what provides the necessary growth. If the lessons aren't learned, they are bound to repeat in your life until you see their meaning and can move on.

For that, we thank the ones that have crossed our paths, at times making us weaker but, in the end, making us stronger. Facing the unknown is the first step to becoming your own best friend and having a Hopeful Mind.

With much love from Jana and Lesia

Dedication

I dedicate this to my husband, John Baron, who has been by my side through thick and thin and supported me every step of the way. I don't know what I would have done without you and I am glad I didn't have to find out.

Much love always. Jana

Dedication

The word "hopeful" is very clear in my mind because I was blessed to have two parents that were the best I could have asked for. I remain *hopeful* that although our time together has passed on this earth, that we will meet again one day, so I can tell them how fortunate I was to have had such wonderful role models.

I remain ever so hopeful that we will meet again but if we don't, I want to dedicate this book to Maksym and Olga Kluczkowski for being the best in so many ways. I love you both and miss you, more than you can imagine, every single day.

With love and hope always that we will meet again one day.

Your loving daughter, Lesia.

ABUNDANCE

A is for Abundance

*"Riches are not from abundance
of worldly goods,
but from a contented mind."* – Unknown

Abundance: A very large quantity of something or plentifulness of the good things of life.

I believe this could refer to tangible items like owning 1,000 books (guilty as charged). It is also the intangible things in life that you can have in abundance, such as fulfilling work or love and support of friends or family.

The opposite of abundance to me is lack and that can be a little tricky because it's a matter of perception. Many people would focus on a lack of money but that lack may only be because of a desire to "want" as opposed to "need" more.

If you compared yourself to one part of the world, you would see that you have much abundance with money. If you view yourself and your life compared to a different group, you could consider yourself lacking or in need.

If you were truly honest with yourself, would you say you had an abundance or lack as it relates to your life and lifestyle at this time or is there really enough for what you currently need?

So, I ask you to consider these questions:

Where in your life do you wish to have abundance?

Is it really true that there is a lack in that area?

It's human nature to want more – but do you truly need more?

We drive ourselves to do more so we can have more and, in the end, we witness others fighting over what's left. True fulfillment is being happy where you are now with what you have now by enjoying the present. I'm not saying don't strive for a better life but be happy while you are doing it. Just sayin'!!

A STORY OF ABUNDANCE

Over the years Jimmy collected screwdrivers, not intentionally, it just happened. He continued to add to his collection, year after year, accumulating many different types of screwdrivers.

    Knowing he had so many screwdrivers, when a family member or friend needed one, he would happily pass one on.

    As time went on, his supply went down but he still passed them out as the need arose. Perhaps in his mind he thought his supply was never ending.

    Then one day, Jimmy needed a screwdriver for a project of his own. He searched and he searched and he could not find a single screwdriver. It didn't matter where he looked, there were no screwdrivers. After years of passing them out, Jimmy had to go out and buy one for his own use.

    Abundance of something takes the pressure off of having to purchase that item. If you're not careful and aware of the abundance, it can slowly turn to lack. Remember to keep your eye on the prize so you don't leave yourself short in the end.

BELIEFS

B is for Beliefs

*"Beliefs are choices.
First, you choose your beliefs.
Then, your beliefs affect your choices."
Roy T. Bennett*

Beliefs: Something believed. An opinion or conviction

Most of our actions and how we live our lives align with what we have heard and taken on as our truth. You hear a familiar phrase. It brings forward a memory of a negative comment you heard somewhere in your past. It instantly reels you back to the first time someone said it. In a flash you are transported back to that moment years ago. The comment creates a trigger and you are right back there.

Our thoughts, which create our beliefs, are extremely powerful. Whether they are true or not, we believe them and because we do, we live our lives according to those ideas. I have seen it time and time again. I have even felt it myself. For years, we behave as if something is true even though we know in our hearts it is not.

I recently heard Paul O'Mahony call it our BS– not what you were thinking – but it is, kind of the same. He refers to "BS" as our Belief System.

As an example, a child gets hurt playing and a well-meaning parent tries to make the child less fearful saying "Oh it's not so bad" or "Don't be a crybaby." The belief is planted that we are a crybaby if we cry. The way our brains work is, it continues to look for confirmation that the comment is true. And, our brain does find it. We are "sensitive", "easily-upset", "weak" or whatever other words we hear. Confirmation!!

They are saying it so, it must be true, right?

In order to get rid of any belief, you have to convince your mind that the belief is false but, how do you do that?

It's simple. You give it proof.

1. Think of a comment that you can feel yourself react to when you hear it. What's the comment? What's the belief behind it? Write it down in a notebook.

2. Then think of every reason it's not true. Then write those reasons down. Prove to yourself that it's not true.

For example, if you often heard that you couldn't do a certain job because you weren't qualified, or you weren't smart enough or educated enough. Then think of a time when you know you stepped up and were effective and successful.

This is the proof your brain requires in order to change the pattern and quit putting so much weight on someone else's idea

3. Now read it to yourself three times a day for at least a week. This is how you retrain your brain to see that you have what it takes. I know you can do it.

CHANGES

C is for Changes

*"Yesterday I was clever,
so I wanted to change the world.
Today I am wise, so I am changing myself."*
Rumi

Changes: To transform or convert. To become different, altered or modified.

I thought when I reached this stage of my life, most major changes would be over. How very naïve of me!! Covid-19 anyone? It's 2020 and the world is a different place.

I had a trip booked to San Diego in May of 2020. I was taking my best friend, the best support I could ever imagine in the work that I do, on a trip to thank her for her support of me. Now ... we can't cross the border to catch the flight and, as eventually, the flight was cancelled. "It's the thought that counts" really sucks as I had been planning this surprise for three years. The wine tour was booked. A grand hotel in San Diego was booked. We were thrilled to be going.

This was not a change I would have ever expected. This was tough because my dream of thanking her went up in smoke and I had no control over the outcome.

Life is always changing. People change, people get sick, people leave, people die and, if we have people in our lives, how can our lives not change? This experience with the trip has taught me one thing. It's the people that are still the most important thing. The trip may or may not happen but our friendship still stands. That's more important than anything else. We remain hopeful for the future because the alternative isn't so appealing.

I have heard a phrase lately that really struck me. People talk of their "new normal". What's a new normal? I believe a new normal is a time when something has changed in your life and you have to make adjustments. Doesn't that happen all the time? I know this feels so much bigger and out of our hands but I have to believe that when we look in the rearview mirror, things often improve.

We have experienced recently what it was like to be without people around us. Trip or no trip, I would rather opt for dealing with the changes and having the people that are important around me, for whatever time we have. Wouldn't you?

It's been more difficult for those that have lost loved ones or have endured sickness that has been so debilitating.

I know of a couple that have been married for seventy years. They are wonderful people that still have their full capacities. One is now in a nursing home because of physical limitations and one is in the hospital for the same thing. So, they remain apart, after so many years together. Something feels so very wrong with that.

All of these people that have had to be separated reminds me of the movie "The Titanic" where the couple know full well the boat is going down. You see a shot of them holding on to each other lying on the bed as the water continues to rise.

I wonder what my choice would be at that time when faced with the same circumstances.

Change is here and change will continue forever in our lives. I think with change, the most harmful thing you can do is lose hope. Hope for a brighter day once again. Hope to hold loved ones and once again, eat, drink and most of all, be merry. And in the words of Red Green "We're all in this together."

DISCOVER

D is for Discover

"There are two great days in a person's life. The day we are born and the day we discover why." William Barclay

Discover: *To see, find, or become aware of (something) for the first time.*

Women do for others really well but, not so well, do women do for themselves.

What I've "discovered" over time in working mostly with women is this. There comes a time when many of the duties they have had over the years are not needed to the same extent they were in the past.

For example, the time when you are no longer a parent to the same degree as before. Or, a time, when you retire and, your definition of being a "worker" no longer applies. It's no longer 9 to 5 and it's a change in routine.

Possibly, when you are doing all you can as a caregiver and the day comes when those responsibilities end.

As a result, it can become a time of uncertainty, even some emptiness. Loneliness might creep in and a loss of direction for some.

It is at that point you may look around and feel at loose ends. It doesn't happen to everyone but I have seen it happen to many. I know and understand the feeling because it happened to me for very different reasons. Part of my coming to terms with it was journaling and writing my first book, *"Soul Fire Café, Making Peace with the One in the Mirror"*.

What I have discovered is this. It can also be a time of awakening. A time to re-acquaint yourself with the things you loved, but have put away, for whatever reason. Perhaps something you never had time for because of those other duties. It can be a time when you have an opportunity to rediscover who you are or, remember who you were. Then, you can embrace who you want to be, going forward.

If that feels difficult, it may only be a little fear standing in your way. It's quite normal actually because it's unfamiliar and you may not know where to start. Just remember you only have to take one tiny step at a time. Take the step. See where it leads.

If you are at this point and it's time to discover the real you, then take the opportunity to examine things. You might like what you find. You may even reconnect with an old hobby or reignite your creativity and start one.

At the very least, you may meet someone you haven't seen in a long while. Be sure to smile and say "Hello Old Friend. Won't you come in?". I'm pretty sure you'll be glad you did.

EMPATHY

E is for Empathy

"Never look down on another person unless you are helping them up." Jesse Jackson

Empathy: The ability to share another person's feelings and emotions as if they were your own.

I was very privileged to see empathy in action. While taking a course, I witnessed an amazing display of empathy by our instructor. Our facilitator, (let's call him Jim), was having breakfast before heading into a full day of working with our group. He spotted a gentleman who appeared completely distraught. Most people would just watch out of the corner of their eye to see if they could figure out what was wrong. More often than not, they wouldn't get involved.

As if feeling his pain, (the very definition of empathy), Jim did get involved. He reached out, not wanting to intrude but, out of genuine concern. He checked with him to see if he was okay. The man motioned for Jim to have a seat.

He proceeded to tell Jim he had just found out that his child had died through the night in another City. The man was in terrible distress as you might imagine. He was completely at a loss as to how to process what had happened. He was also alone and Jim was the ear he needed at that moment.

After listening, Jim was able to provide some assistance to get him to a position where he had some help. The man was so grateful and his stress level subsided enough for him to be able to do what needed to be done next. I can't imagine what would have happened to this man had Jim not bothered to speak to him.

The display of care Jim showed this stranger was absolutely wonderful to witness. I will never forget it.

The next time you see someone in distress, maybe take a moment and see if you can be the "ear" they need. You could be the one thing that makes a difference.

We are so busy living our lives, running around in a frenzy, thinking about everything on our priority list as if it's the only thing in this world that is important. It isn't.

You never really know what is happening in someone else's world at a given time. Maybe your smile will give them the courage to do what they need to do that day. A smile that tells them they aren't invisible. Someone saw them and that could be a turning point in their lives.

We all carry our own burdens and they are invisible to everyone else. There was a time when someone bit my head off at work and, initially, I took offense to it. When I asked someone, I discovered it was the anniversary of her son's death. The entire interaction gave me a completely different perspective and I knew I shouldn't take it personally. People hurt for many reasons. Sometimes it just means you were at the wrong place at the wrong time.

Try a little empathy. It can go a long way to helping you and the other person get over a hurdle and feel better. All it takes is taking a moment to stop instead of reacting instantaneously. It's not always about us.

FEAR

F is for Fear

"F.E.A.R. - Feel Emotion and Release"
Lesia Zablockij

Fear: To feel apprehensive or uneasy about a situation, whether the threat is real or imagined.

I have come to understand fear as living in the "What ifs?". As time passes, most often the "What if this happens?" or "What if that happens?" or "What if that doesn't happen?" is that they usually don't. We waste our precious time hiding under the dark cloud of "what if?" which ends up being a huge waste of time and energy. Humans are a pretty resilient bunch, even when we don't think we are. We tackle many things that come our way and we survive most of them.

Fear is simply an emotion. It is an emotion to protect us, which is a good thing. What we have to watch is that the emotion doesn't protect us from things that are harmless. It can stop us from accomplishing things that we want or would be good for us.

What if I lose my job? What if I can't handle the changes in the world? What if we don't survive this? Many of us are fearful of our current reality. It's a scary time. The world is always changing and we have little control.

The things that scare us the most are the things that help us grow. The fear of losing a job might just be an opening to an opportunity you have wanted or something you may not be aware of at the moment. It may not happen immediately but being open to the possibilities is not a bad thing. I tend to believe there's a plan out there for us and, if we can stop fighting it long enough to let it happen, we might all be a little *less* stressed. It could be possible.

We can't stop ourselves from worrying so allow it, for a short time. Then change your focus. Trust that you have the inner resources to weather the storms and be open to set sail when the time comes.

Our entire world is different right now but that doesn't mean we throw up our hands and say "whatever" or "why bother?". We need to bother. We need to care and we need to do the best we can. We are being asked to make sacrifices for the time being. My co-author said to me "We are making sacrifices to stay home for Christmas this year so we can all be at the table next year." I absolutely love that simple but significant statement. Can we not do for each other now so our future is a little brighter?

I understand worrying but instead of worrying all day, try and see what little thing you might be able to do for a neighbour or a friend. Drop off a small bag of groceries or send someone who lives alone a pizza. It would brighten up the day for both of you I'm pretty sure.

Nothing has to be a grand gesture. Even a phone call to check in on someone is a good thing. So many people are alone right now that a moment of personal connection would be welcomed in most cases. What can you do today to bring a little sunshine?

GRATEFUL

G is for Grateful

"Gratitude turns what we have into enough."
Unknown

Grateful: Deeply appreciative or thankful for the kindness or benefits received.

When we look around and feel the fear and insecurity of what's next in our world, what we are really looking for is a sense of certainty and some peace in our hearts. We are all in the same boat and putting the focus on things like gratitude can help us through the turmoil we feel.

I once asked if you had one week left to live, what would you do with that time? What I realized is that, during our time of isolation, I was probably already doing exactly what I would be doing if I had one week to live. Perhaps the way we do those things has changed but, we have found a way to connect, and I am so very grateful for that.

I have managed to spend considerable time in the same room with my husband and that's what I would have done. The 1% that may have been slightly unpleasant doesn't hold a candle to the 99% that has been good.

I have stayed connected to people I care about having "wine dates" on the phone or on Zoom.

I have read with my great-nephew and we have shared a few giggles on Zoom more than before this interruption of life.

I have had telephone conversations with my niece and had many laughs.

I have joined the residents of our condo for Tuesday afternoon symphony in the halls. All this while social distancing and listening to a piano at the end of the hall, playing many oldies but goodies.

In all of that, I was grateful. Grateful that I woke up to have another day. Grateful that the people I love are still here. Grateful that they still want to talk to me.

It's about perspective. There's a lot happening out there but it's like focusing my camera on Zoom. I choose the view. You can too.

Gratitude has a lot to do with perspective in my opinion. Reminds me of the glass half-empty or half full. It's simply the way you look at it. With all the conspiracy theories that have been flying around and all the negativity that could certainly take over one's life fairly easily, I choose to not spend my time being consumed by it.

We all have our ideas and opinions about what's happening this year and that's a good thing. We should have our own opinions. However, there are very few that truly know the plan, assuming there is one.

In the meantime, be grateful. Grateful you have been granted another day. Grateful that you can still speak to the ones you love. Grateful for the many that are working so hard to keep everyone healthy and alive. Also, even grateful for the ones that are long gone and did not have to go through this. It's the little blessings that are important during difficult times. If you look hard enough, I'm sure you can find them.

HOPE

H is for Hope

"Hope is being able to see that there is light despite all of the darkness." **Desmond Tutu**

Hope: The feeling that what is wanted can be had or that events will turn out for the best.

The world is spinning and will never be the same. There is so much flying around out there that we question what's true, what's hype, what's just mis-information and what are just out-and-out lies. I don't have the answers and I doubt I ever will.

Of course, Black Lives matter. All lives matter. They always have. I wasn't raised to think differently about other races. I know my parents were immigrants after the war and were so happy to be here that they embraced everyone. I shudder to think how they would feel if they were around to see what's going on now.

What I do know is what I see in my backyard. I work with a lawyer from an African nation. I have nothing but respect for this individual. I don't see colour. I see a person. No different than me.

I see friends helping out their neighbours, again a family from an African nation. They don't see colour. They are always ready to help them out with their responsibilities as new homeowners.

All I can say is, if they were in need, none of us would walk away. That's our world and we are comfortable in it.

During lockdown, I have had time to go through many boxes that sat waiting for "that day" that I could finally go through them. I have no boxes left to sift through – they are now empty and I couldn't feel more at peace.

I ran across many memories, happier times, reminders of people that once played an important part in my life. Some are gone and buried. Others just buried. I read every card I had kept and the love that was poured into them. Some still mean it. Others, well, not so much. That's life. I kept the ones that still held meaning.

What I did find is my own "**I Have a Dream**" speech that I had written many years ago. It just seems fitting to share now.

I have a dream:
- to live in a world where people respect each other
- where people aren't afraid to love
- where people value life and take time to appreciate each other
- where kindness isn't regarded suspiciously
- and where people stop and think before they destroy the sense of wonder in a child.

    I still live in hope of that dream. If you have a similar hope, try to not lose sight of it. It may be the single thing that helps you make it through the day, the week, the month or the year. When we look back, we will think "Oh what a year that was!". I doubt there will be much wishing "If I could just do that year over again." I think we will be unified in not wanting that to happen. There's something to hope for. All of us being united in our hope to not do a do-over of 2020. Maybe it's a stretch but, I will hold on to my hope any way I can.

INSPIRATION

I is for Inspiration

"There is no greater agony than bearing an untold story inside you." Maya Angelou

Inspiration: To produce or awaken a feeling, thought, idea or action.

Inspiration is wonderful, especially when you are able to share it with someone. That has been a little more challenging these days but, is it enough to feel inspired yourself? I believe it is.

I have been on a journey and found inspiration all along the way. Every once in a while, I have to dig a little deeper. When it comes to writing, once I have the idea, I have been fortunate enough to have the writing flow fairly easily. Inspiration is still the key. If I don't have a bit of an idea in my head to start with, I can get stuck as easily as the next person.

Today, I wanted to share something more personal. I have been a writer all of my life. As a teenager I won a national writing contest and they actually paid me! I was amazed. Paid to put a few words on a piece of paper? Unbelievable.

Life went on and I put my writing to the side. It wasn't until I had to dig myself out of a very dark place, that I started to write again. It was one of the things that saved me and I haven't stopped since.

Writing inspires me. My journey inspires me. It's not over yet, so I will continue to write.

Whether you enjoy painting, drawing, making original greeting cards, gardening or whatever lights you up, do it. Do it now. Time doesn't stop and, if it's something you love, map out time for it.

I have few regrets in life. One is what I could have written had I not let life get in the way. Now, I write every week. Let your mind create. That's what it's for.

If you feel inspired to write a song, sing a song, play an instrument, be a poet, a painter or a dancer, make time for it. Whatever that thing is that whispers so quietly in your ear, the thing that makes you light up, pay attention to it. It could be guiding you to a place you've never been but need to go. If only for the experience, it's worth it, to take a look at what's calling to you.

You know those times when you say "I always wanted to learn piano" or whatever it is for you. Just do it. I was watching a show where one of the cast members was feeling she didn't have a "thing". She didn't feel the connection to anything and she felt out of sorts about it, perhaps even less than. She tried and she tried and, eventually, she found the connection. When she got that connection, the smile on her face was as big as it could be. She felt the inspiration and it made her happy and it could do the same for you. Come on – give it a try. You just might surprise yourself.

JOURNAL

J is for Journal

"Journal writing is a voyage to the interior."
Christina Baldwin

Journal: To write self-examining or reflective entries into a notebook.

To journal or not to journal …

Are you successful at journaling?

What's this journaling all about? It has become very popular over the years.

I have created a five year, a three year and a weekly journal. In all honesty, I have tried to write in all of them, as well as others, but have not yet succeeded in making it anything more than sporadic. I am a writer so I really don't get that!

Two friends in particular, one male, one female, are on Year 17 using the books I have made for them. It simply amazes me and I am honored!

My five-year journals have the same day on each page for five years. By the time you get to the end, you can reflect on the last five years. I originally had a quote on each page.

Every 5 years, I set out to find 366 new quotes. There was also a line for what we are thankful for each day. I had passed them out initially as a gift to friends. A few went to new parents to document their child's first five years.

They can reflect on how far they have come, the lessons they have learned (or not), how much life changes and, also, how we are creatures of habit. An example is, two of us went to the same mall on the same Saturday for several years. Not planned but when you can look back, you can see the pattern.

It shows the celebrations, the highlights, the people you shared your life with, here and gone. You see how relationships have flourished or fallen apart and you grow to understand what past relationships were all about.

I can only surmise that if they still journal after 17 years, it has some value for them. For that, I am truly grateful I played a small part.

If you haven't had a chance to read Matthew McConaughey's book "Greenlights", it's worth a read. He wrote his book because of notes he made while he journaled for the past

35 years. That is a true testament to what journaling can help you achieve. He has snippets from his journals in the book and it's really interesting to read.

I know from the people that write in the journals I made, there is a wealth of reminders, good memories, happy thoughts and perhaps a few not so happy ones. You choose what you put in the journal. It can be something you are grateful for every day.

It can be used to record milestones, achievements, thoughts of yours at the time. Upon reflection, you can even see that maybe you have reached some of those goals you set for yourself without even knowing it. What a way to celebrate that perhaps you have done more than you think you have.

Alternatively, maybe it's a reminder that there was something else you wanted to try and it has been forgotten. Whatever the reason, journals can be terrific tools and a good friend. They are privy to your deepest thoughts and best ideas. Congratulations Matthew. Way to go!

KEY

K is for Key
(Knowledge Empowers You)

*"The greatest enemy of knowledge is not ignorance,
it is the illusion of knowledge". Daniel J. Boorstin*

Key: Essential, central, important.

I'm not sure when I decided I wanted to keep learning or if it was instilled in me by my parents or teachers. I know I have never stopped.

Being a lifelong learner has helped me and allowed me to help others. The more you learn, the more activity in your brain. It's easy to learn about something that interests you but, if you haven't found anything, you can start by dabbling. Find something you have some curiosity about and look into it. It may be all you need to get your creative juices flowing.

My husband and I have watched a ton of Australian quiz shows. We might even get a tad competitive but, that's okay, it's more interactive that way. From the comfort of our living room and without the expense of travel, we have seen a whole other world we knew little about. The slang of the language is just an example. Like the way they say "yeah" before answering a simple question such as "how you GOING?" (another example). I have found it's just a different way of learning.

I have worked with people who were lost, unmotivated or stuck. There are any number of reasons why that happens to people. I discovered I don't need to understand all the ways it happens. What I do need to understand, is how to access it with them. That's the KEY and that's one of the things I keep learning.

What I have found is people suspect they know the reason. Often it is something different. With the right key, we can unearth the nail that continues to scratch below the surface. They may have been able to ignore it until something triggers it and each time it gets harder to push back down. That really is okay because it needs to get up and out of your system so you can move on without the anchor.

Without the access key, the truth remains hidden and continues to stand in the way. Give it some attention, free yourself and by all means, reach for help if you need it.

There is no shame to ask for help. You are worth it.

    The key is always the way in and we don't always have access to the key ourselves. But once you turn that key, your whole world can change for the better. I recall a story about a person sitting on a chair in the middle of a locked room. They look around and couldn't figure out why they were stuck or how to escape. What they don't realize is they are the only one that holds the key. They may not be able to get to it, but it truly is within their reach. They just need to do one of two things. One would be to sit back and look inward instead of fighting to find a way outside of themselves. The second is to find someone to assist them in accessing it. Either way, finding the key is what gives you the freedom to once again fly.

LOQUACIOUS

L is for Loquacious

"The trouble with her is that she lacks the power of conversation but not the power of speech." George Bernard Shaw

Loquacious: Talking or tending to talk too much or too freely; talkative; chattering; babbling; garrulous.

I miss conversation. I miss people's voices, laughter and their lilt. I miss hearing people's stories. I miss just finding out how people are doing these days. It's been too long and I truly miss it.

I was watching a couple at a restaurant with their son. The couple is familiar to me and the husband is usually pretty quiet. I watched the father chatting up a blue streak this particular day, totally out of character. The son was glued to his phone. He may have grunted out a word here or there but he didn't look up from his phone.

It also reminded me of a client who was suffering because of the times he chose to avoid his own father and, unfortunately, that choice no longer exists because he is no longer here.

Sometimes you yearn for peace and quiet. I get it. I am perfectly fine with spending some alone time. I don't mind my own company. I do, however, miss people and conversation.

As I watched this young man at the restaurant not even look up to thank the waitress when she brought his dinner, I wondered what our next generation was going to be like. These young adults may become parents in the future if they can put their phones aside long enough. What will become of the art of conversation; will it no longer exist? To me, that's a horrible reality. We have mastered the art of language and no longer grunt at each other in caves. Are we going forward with technology and going backward with life? I often think about these things and wonder what is to be. We are always advancing but it shouldn't be at the cost of things that are important like relationships and connection.

So, I urge you all to be loquacious. We need to hear words. We need to engage with one another. Start a conversation. Stop and smile, even if it's through your mask at this time. Your eyes do light up and people can see those.

Above all, please talk to each other. I have been asked some questions about the past recently that if you don't find out while you can, it may be too late. I know my husband and I both regret that we didn't ask more about our parent's history. You think there's always time but no one really knows how much time we have.

So, talk, ask questions, tell people you care about how much they mean to you and why you cherish their presence in your life. Tell them now, before you can't, so you don't live in regret in the future. It's really not that hard. Put the device down and have a chat. You might actually enjoy it and learn something.

MEMORIES

M is for Memories

*"The worst part of holding the memories is not the pain.
It's the loneliness of it.
Memories need to be shared."* **Lois Lowry**

Memories: A mental impression retained; a recollection.

How different a time it is for making memories! Our get-togethers are limited, the places we visit are limited, the hugs, seeing smiles or even tears of those we care about, is limited.

That doesn't mean that we can't make different types of memories.

I was looking at my dear friend's scrapbook tributes she makes for her grandchildren. They truly are works of art. Pictures, notes and mementoes, unique for each of her five grandchildren. What a beautiful memory she creates.

One of my favourite memories was reading to my great-nephew on Zoom. I accidentally slammed my finger into the wall and crap it hurt! He has just turned 8 and laughed and asked me why I did that? Well, how do you explain that to the little guy. I told him I didn't know where my arms ended! So, a little memory was made that I still laugh and shake my head about.

This is a time that will be forever ingrained in our minds but it doesn't all have to be negative. What I have seen is how people have become amazingly creative.

- The car parades with flags and posters wishing people Happy Birthday.
- The grad celebrations that have continued in new and interesting ways.
- Even a weekly music get-together that was shut down but reconvened in a park.
- We even did food exchanges from the street with friends cause heck there was a lot of baking going on at my friend's house.

Memories are different but they are still memories. We will remember this time clearly so let's make sure there are good ones mixed in the bunch. I have spent my time purging, realizing how little I truly need to survive.

I wanted to share a few lyrics from the musical "Cats".

Memory, all alone in the moonlight.
I can dream of the old days, life was beautiful then.
I remember, the time I knew what happiness was.
Let the memory live again.

    It doesn't matter what is happening in the world at any given time. Memories are always forming. Good things still happen. Laughter still happens. If we put our focus on the things that bring us joy it can help while we struggle through whatever is going on at the present time. We can still be silly. We can still care about others.

    There was a movie several years ago that won several awards called "Life is Beautiful". It was a story about a Jewish man and his son as they become victims of the Holocaust. He is separated from his son but they can hear each other.

    The father uses imagination to protect his son from the reality of the situation by making it a game. He continually talks to the son and creates scenarios that make whatever is going on at the time to be part of the game and be less traumatic for the son.

    I can't imagine anything making that situation any lighter but, in this movie, the father did. I think if we try hard, we can make this situation easier instead of harder too, even if it just makes each day a little brighter.

NORMAL

N is for Normal

"Normal's just a setting on the washing machine". *Bernice Lewis song*

Normal: Conforming to the standard type; usual; not abnormal.

What the heck is Normal these days? We hear a lot about the "new normal" but I'm not sure I'm liking it much.

It feels like one day is the same as the one before. Nothing new happening. Nothing much to talk about. I feel like I have already entered the senior's home to await the inevitable.

Normal ... I'm not sure anything is normal anymore. When I think back to what my parents and maybe some of yours lived through, that was much worse than this new normal.

My parents survived World War II. They left their country. They left their families, most never to be seen again. I never met my grandparents or most of my aunts or uncles.

They came to Canada with my oldest brother, a single trunk and each other. I still have the trunk in my living room with their name and the date they arrived in Canada.

    My parents sent me to Ukraine in the 1980's and, unbeknownst to me, my mother's sister and family, came to my hotel and found me. I didn't even have to be introduced. I looked at her face in the lobby and I instantly knew. I hadn't seen her picture but I saw my mother's face in her and I simply knew. It was one of the most amazing moments of my life.

    So, as sorry as I feel for myself on some days and, I do, I can't even imagine making a choice to walk away from everything that meant anything in my life and creating what was their new normal. Quite frankly what is being asked of us is not such a big sacrifice.

    Sure, things are kind of boring and repetitive and, I miss hugging up people that I love. Hopefully that will pass in time and we can reunite and embrace.

    For now, for us, for the human race, we need to be safe and live this new normal a little while longer. I think we should all be able to do that for each other.

My co-author said to be "we sacrifice today so we can all be together in the new year". I thought that was such a good way to look at it. We want as many of us to be safe and healthy as possible. I think it's worth it.

I know some of our freedoms seem to be out of reach but if trying to be safe keeps me looking down at the ground instead of up at it, I think I can adjust to this new normal for a while longer. I'm really hoping you can too.

ONLY

O is for Only

"Life is only a flicker of melted ice."
Dejan Stojanovic

Only: Without others or anything further; solely; alone; exclusively.

We use the phrase "if only" interchangeably with "when" but in a less committed way. When we say "when", it sounds like you mean it. "If only" is more questionable which leads me to working with deadlines. "If only" is much more fluid which often means "when*ever*". It definitely has for me.

Have you ever said any of these things?

If only, I could lose 20, 30, 40 … lbs.

If only I hadn't gone out until ….

If only, I had been there.

If only, I hadn't been too afraid to …

If only, I hadn't doubted …

If only, I had saved more …

If only, I hadn't stopped at …

If only, they hadn't seen me …

"If onlys" are statements of regret. It's looking back and wishing things were different. Wishing things were different is one of the underlying reasons people struggle with grief. They think they have lost a piece of themselves but that's not the case. I'm not suggesting it doesn't feel that way, it's just not really true. What really happens is regret holds a piece of us hostage. It needs to be released in order to feel whole again. You are always whole but there are just times when it doesn't feel that way.

Although grief is caused by many things, death is mostly what people relate it to. We all know, logically, that none of us are getting out of here alive. So, let's stop our "if onlys" and use "whens" or "nows".

The best way to live your life is, without regret. We make choices and decisions based on the information and knowledge we had at the time. Isn't it time to accept that and stop beating yourself up about it?

We don't know what lies ahead so why not make the best of it. Our decisions are based on the cards that are laid out at a specific moment in time. We don't know what tomorrow brings. If we did, we might make an entirely different decision but we don't know what comes tomorrow or next week. We truly shouldn't blame ourselves for making a decision on the facts that we have at hand. It's the best we can do.

Let's say for example, the weather forecast is for a warm, sunny day so we head out of the City for a drive with only a light jacket and sandals. On the way back, a snowstorm hits so bad that we have to pull over until it passes because we can't see clearly. We based our decision on the information that the weather channel provided. How could we have known there would be such a storm? It's a simplistic example but it does prove a point. Try and not be so hard on yourself for going with the only information you had at the time you made the decision and stop the "If only …".

Hmmm – "If only" I had a crystal ball …

PLANNING

P is for Planning

"Life is what happens to us while we are making other plans."
Allen Saunders

Planning: The act or process of making a plan.

Planning sounds so strange these days. What are we planning for or, how do you make any plans make sense? I wish I had a panacea to heal our world but sadly, there is no magic pill to solve the dilemmas of today.

We can still make plans though. They will be different for many of us but we can still move ahead. Once government assistance stops and, it will, we will have to make plans but why wait until we are forced to do so.

We will still have to earn a living if we want to survive. Education is already changing gears. Online courses have been around for a long time but they are certainly becoming more popular and accessible. Athabasca University has offered online courses for years now. It's not new.

Even though our future is uncertain as to how things will play out, it will still play out in some way.

So, why not get ahead of the curve as they say. Make your plans or, at least make the plans you can. Keep moving ahead, even if it's just a baby step. Ask yourself, what one thing can I do today to move myself forward towards a future I want? Things like, giving your resume a once over. Brushing up on your skills online while you are stuck at home.

How about going through your wardrobe and "stuff" to clear the way for something good to come in. I don't know much about Feng Shui but I'm sure there is a reason for clearing to make an entrance for other things.

I continue to work on my business and am adding skills that interest me. What's your baby step today? Tomorrow? The next day? This part really is still in our control so why not take advantage of what you can instead of waiting for life to happen to you.

Somewhere along the way someone said to pick your top 3 items to do each day. It may have been business-related but I think you could also use it for personal reasons as well.

What 3 things could you do each day to keep you moving forward? It could be a simple as try on three pairs of pants. Covid has made pant sizes vary a little over the past year. Don't hang on to the ones that make you feel like you never want to leave the house again. That won't do much for your self-esteem or, mood, for that matter.

I'm sure you can come up with 3 things that might be a little more exciting than that but it's a start. I know this may be easier for some than for others but I'm sure if you look hard enough, there are baby steps we can all take in making our lives a little easier.

What will your 3 things be?

QUAGMIRE

Q is for Quagmire

"I didn't realize this was a sad occasion."
Lemony Snicket

Quagmire: An awkward, complex or hazardous situation.

I really think this is a good way to describe the position we are in at this time. I have been feeling pretty stuck and quite tired of this. The new term is "COVID Fatigue" and I know I feel it. It's the connection that I miss as I have said before.

I was trying to describe it as feeling like I'm stuck in one place, like running on the spot, not that I've ever done much of that.

I think about the time the children are losing in education and socialization. We have to equip them as best we can for whatever their future holds. We live in fear about exposure if they return to school but it takes 21 days to form a habit. What habits are these long months creating for all of us?

Entrepreneurship is on the rise with some people having the best months of their careers in business. Other establishments are finding it difficult getting staff to return to work as they have an income without working.

Every generation has its struggles and we seem to manage to make it through somehow. Always a new challenge. I truly hope this too shall pass and we come out of it stronger but it's feeling pretty boggy at the moment.

My biggest concern is what if stores stop making pants. We've seen reporters working from home with pyjama bottoms and a jacket and tie. I still want to be able to buy pants!

Quagmires show up often but this one seems like a doozy because we are entrenched in it right now. I guess we can just continue to hope that we don't follow the path of Quagmire from Family Guy and develop his addiction to sketchy material. I think if we just stay the course, develop a hobby or do something that will ease the pain of it all, we should come out of it okay.

I know the biggest complaint we often have is there's not enough time to do it all. We have the time. Are you using it to *"git'r'done?"* *(thank you Larry The Cable Guy).* If not, maybe we need to think about that and, in the future, stop complaining about not having time. Time is probably not the problem. Maybe it's motivation or ... lack thereof.

Now back to pants. Among other things, 2020 may be remembered as the year pants become optional and not mandatory. All I ask is that you promise me that you will try at least to remember the undies. It gets a bit chilly in Canada in the winter and you don't want to get frosticles.

RAUCOUS

R is for Raucous

"Sometimes silence can be the loudest thing."
Ellie Mathews

Raucous: Rowdy, disorderly.

Raucous is often used to refer to loud laughter, loud voices, or a loud party, all of which can be harsh or unpleasant.

Don't you just miss the loud laughter and loud voices? It seems there hasn't been much of that or, at least, not enough for my liking.

I have a loud laugh. I remember when I was first married, my husband would try to tone me down (ever so gently). I don't recall being overly loud but heck, if you are going to laugh, why would you do it quietly?

I love a "belly laugh" – so loud and deep you can feel it in your toes.

There are few things more therapeutic than a good, deep laugh. I believe it has a healing power all on its own.

Today I have decided to tell you a joke in the hopes it will make you laugh and laugh loudly. I rarely remember jokes but for some reason I always loved this one.

A kindergarten teacher is trying to teach her young students about flavours; colours and taste. As a teaching aide, she used lifesavers and had them try each one.

First, there was a lemon one, then an orange one, then a cherry one. The kids were doing really well guessing all of them without a problem. The teacher then gave them one that was honey-flavoured and the kids were having a really hard time trying to figure it out.

Seeing their frustration, the teacher said "Okay, I'll give you a hint. It's something your parents may call each other at home."

From the back of the room, you see little Johnny jump to his feet and yell "Spit them out, spit them out. They're a**holes."

Sorry if you find that in bad taste but it makes me laugh every time I think about it. I can just picture Little Johnny, can't you? What a household little Johnny must have grown up in.

I hope that made you laugh too. Let's try and not let the bad attitudes out there take away our joy and laughter. Sometimes, it's all that keeps us sane.

Focusing on the news can bring you right down so limiting that time is not a bad thing. My suggestion is to add in some time to read or watch a comedy or even a chic flick. See kindness and caring. Have some giggles and try to get some balance. Listening to negativity all the time can do unhealthy things to one's mind. Try to take it up a notch or two by bringing some levity to your day. You know "let's turn that frown upside down". Sorry, I just had to say it. I hope it made you smile.

STORY

S is for Story

"But how could you live and have no story to tell?"
Fyodor Dostoevsky

Story: A narration of a chain of events, either fact or fiction.

What's Your Story? We all have one!

We live and breathe our stories. Sometimes we even carry them as a badge of honour.

In my fifteen years of working with clients, listening to friends and listening to co-workers, the stories are all different, that is for sure. Sometimes the stories are true. Sometimes we get creative and get them to mean something completely different.

Our life stories are also very different from one another. It doesn't matter how many were in your family, whether you were a single child or had ten siblings. There is not one family that has the same dynamic as another. We talk about "the black sheep", "the middle child", "the golden boy" or "the rebel", to name a few. But even in those confines, each one is different.

The thing is we have the choice to let our stories, real or not, guide our way. You have heard of people breaking the cycle or, of those that have succeeded against all odds. Those are the ones that chose a different road than their story, or the path the version of their story may have taken them down.

It's not always easy and, it takes some chops, to put yourself or yours ahead of others and make different choices.

I have seen first-hand what family can create in a child's life. I have witnessed some succumb and bury themselves in complacency believing this is all there is. I have also seen others strive, regardless of the crap that was handed to them. To those I say Bravo. To the rest I say, it's never too late to choose a new path.

We get an idea of what we want and where we want to be. If we don't get there, we can create any number of reasons to explain why we didn't succeed. It takes guts to examine if those stories are really true or, if they were just excuses, for why we may have failed.

Failing also is in our eyes and in our stories. If we give up, we may never know how the story might have ended. If we make a choice to stop for whatever reason, then that's a choice we make to end this part of the story.

You have heard the one about the person leaning a ladder against a wall and when he has finished climbing it discovers it was leaning against the wrong wall. This only shows that maybe, just maybe, the path wasn't quite taking you where you were meant to go and perhaps, it may be time to move your ladder.

I have a picture hanging in my office which says

"Sometimes your life is defined by a single moment
Let it be Today."

Is today your day to become "tough, tough, tough" and decide that this is your life and your story?

TIME

T is for Time

"Don't waste your time in anger, regrets, worries, and grudges. Life is too short to be unhappy." Roy T. Bennett

"Time in a Bottle by Jim Croce

If I could save time in a bottle
The first thing that I'd like to do
Is to save every day
'Til eternity passes away
Just to spend them with you."

If Only ...

Time: A limited period or interval.

Time is one of those things that only moves forward and will eventually run out. The only way time goes backwards is if that is where we put our focus. It doesn't change anything.

I stay awake often because I can't shut off my mind. I started writing about triggers as my "T" word but decided it was about "time" instead.

I think about time running out a lot more lately than I ever have. I wonder if it's because there are so many things I wanted to do, but haven't yet. Maybe I'm not supposed to do all of them but I thought it was *time* to do something about them or put them aside.

Many years ago, on a trip home from Chicago, my husband and I wrote down 100 things that we would like to do. It's a long drive. I ran across that notebook a while back. I was actually amazed at how many things we were able to cross off. A few were crossed off because the interest was gone but most were crossed off because they were done. Maybe there is something to this writing it down so it will come to pass thing.

So, with this idea of time in my head at 1:00 a.m., I decided to think about writing a new list. The list will be smaller because I don't believe there are that many burning desires left undone. Amazingly, that's not a bad thing.

The things that I think about now are the creative things that I put off probably because they weren't "work-related" and so, as a result, unimportant. I realize that thinking is very flawed. You never know where something will lead you. If the inspiration is in you to be creative in some fashion, it should not be ignored.

I stopped writing for 30 years and starting again just as my Mother was dying. Now two books are published and two journals are published. You are reading the fifth book and the sixth is close to being published. I would have never thought I would publish even one book but I hoped I would be able to publish at least one.

So, I will start my new list and I challenge you to do the same. Let's see how many we can stroke off by the end of this year and, at the beginning of the next year, see what you want to add to it. More than you think may just happen.

UNIQUE

U is for Unique

*"Personality begins where comparison leaves off.
Be unique. Be memorable.
Be confident. Be proud." Shannon L. Alder*

Unique: Having no like or equal; unparalleled; incomparable.

My mind is so weird sometimes. I often marvel at how many versions of people exist with a basic combination of two eyes, one nose and one mouth. Have you ever just stopped and looked around? It is truly amazing.

What's even more astonishing is how our minds all work so differently. We are seeing that all around us now. In the midst of crisis and uncertainty, we all react so differently.

I have spent a considerable amount of time listening to podcasts and seminars over the years. I heard someone recently say about tough times, "first we survive, then we thrive". I think that's true and I certainly hope it's true this time around.

Sometimes, being unique is undervalued. Often, that is because a closed mind can only see things one way, and is not open to the possibility of another way.

We all have gifts. We all have things that are inherently our own to offer to ourselves, to our relationships and to the world. It's been said that the world is suffering from an empathy deficit. I am pretty sure my empathy scale is pretty high. I recall gasping out loud at the end of *The Notebook* because I could so feel the emotion in the movie. It was kind of embarrassing but what could I do?

There is beauty in uniqueness and no one should try and hide it. We were never meant to be the same. As I said in the beginning, take a look around. The differences are obvious but our gifts are less visible unless we allow them to be seen.

Our unique qualities may be a little buried because we have been hurt. It could be because we've become afraid to be embarrassed so we hide. Your gifts are just that. You are you are that alone makes you memorable and, that should be enough to step up and show the world your talents. After all, there is no one else like you in this world. Look around and be proud.

    We are all truly one of a kind. Everyone likes their coffee or their steak in a certain way. Why should we not be our own special mix as well? As long as you aren't hurting someone else, do something daring. Show us your stuff. It just might be the thing that someone else has been looking for and hasn't found, whether it's an employer, a relationship or a friend.

    Stop getting in your own way. Do something you have always wanted to do but held back for whatever reason. Maybe now's the time for you to "Just do you". You know the saying "To thine own self be true". The longest relationship you have in your life is the one with yourself. Why would you begrudge yourself and stay in hiding? Let the real you stand up.

VULNERABILITY

V is for Vulnerability

"To share your weakness is to make yourself vulnerable; to make yourself vulnerable is to show your strength." Criss Jami

Vulnerability: The quality or state of being exposed to the possibility of being attacked or harmed, either physically or emotionally.

It's been hard to write this note. I have come to a point in my life where, for my own sanity, I had to admit to the end of an era but, that's a whole other story. That is why I decided to pick the word vulnerability.

If we all knew the answers to our futures, vulnerability would never be an issue. It's in those moments when you aren't sure of what's behind the next door, or around the corner, that vulnerability creeps in.

Sometimes, because we have that feeling of trepidation, we hold back. Maybe we don't trust because of a previous relationship or, we had a bad experience at a job, so looking for a new one scares us. Hurt is a strong teacher but what if, by holding back or needing to know all the answers to what lies ahead, keeps us small, keeps us alone and keeps us invisible? I don't believe that serves anyone.

If we let our vulnerability make us lose our motivation, that would be disastrous. We feel bad because we have been hurt but most times, the people that have hurt us, I would bet, spend much less time thinking about the incident than we might.

It's okay to be vulnerable; that's how you get over pain. If your ego has been bruised, that too shall pass if you keep persevering and striving. We have all been hurt. Just like the scab that forms over a cut, eventually it falls off and heals what's underneath.

What if we miss out on the love of our life or the best position we could ever hope to have while we continue to lick our wounds? That would be such a terrible shame.

I hope this makes you take another look at where you might be protecting yourself and ask "do I want to continue to live in fear and uncertainty or do I want to take a step and see what waits for me?" I think I know my answer.

Maybe it's time to take that chance. Open up your door, your heart, your mind or even your wallet to allow trust, to embrace love, to learn to cherish and to be generous.

I have been blessed and I have been hurt. I have often said, it's not the end of the road if you are still breathing. I am trying to once again be vulnerable and making room for whatever is coming my way. I hope you do too.

Remember, vulnerability is not a weakness. It is simply showing that you are human. Is there really any other option?

W.T.F.

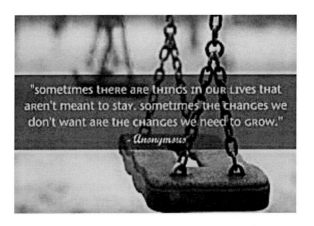

W is for W.T.F.

*"One is never afraid of the unknown;
one is afraid of the known coming to an end."*
Krishnamurti

W.T.F.: I think you got this one!

I'm sure most of us are spinning from the current year. When we feel like we have lost control of our lives, we start to spin. Our focus and attention span suffers and our thoughts are no longer clear.

I read about the growing number of accidents caused by high speeds. Where are we going in such a hurry when there are so few places we should be going? Why are we even on the roads if our minds are so muddled? I certainly don't know the answers but I know I don't relish the thought of being on any highway right now.

We have been asked to take care of ourselves and our fellow man. I don't know if there's a plot behind it all but I do know it's out of my control right now. I can take care of myself and those I care about and that's about it.

It seems that the sooner we do that, the sooner life can go back to some form of normalcy. Hoax, conspiracy theory or not, is it really asking too much to wear a mask, use hand sanitizer and keep our distance for the time being? It's not forever but it seems the longer we don't abide by the rules, the longer this will last.

Now, I don't pretend to know the answers. At times, I'm not even sure what the questions are but, what I do see is, we are failing at our test of humanity. We are all people. Who has the right to say one race is better than another or one belief is superior to another? Maybe it's a pipedream that we will embrace this as a time to go back to some values that serve all of us well. I certainly have seen enough anger and hostility for my lifetime.

Others have lived through much more trying times than this. I know people that hid under tables while bombs exploded around them. I know people that fled their countries out of fear for their lives. I don't think the inconvenience of what is being asked of us can even equate to that.

As I write this and look at the fallen leaves and feel the lowering temperatures, I feel a chill in the air for humanity and it saddens me. I yearn for laughter, for hugs and the kindness of strangers.

So, the circle or the "bubble" becomes small. We stay in our safety nets because we don't know what we will encounter when we step out.

I call myself a recovering Catholic for reasons I won't go into right now but, I pray. I pray that we learn tolerance and acceptance of one another. We are different for a reason and maybe it's time we thought about that. I ask you, is it so wrong to be different?

I don't believe in re-writing history. It's where we learn from our mistakes and hopefully grow. If you erase it, we will never learn or remember.

I don't believe in paying for the mistakes of people that lived long before I walked this earth. I'm sorry but it's not my fault.

I don't believe in hurting someone simply because they don't look like I do.

So, all I can say is W.T.F. people! Isn't it time to stop and look at what we are doing here? I think it is.

X

X is for X

"What we know matters but who we are matters more." Brené Brown

X – A simple letter used at the start of few words but when you really examine it, it has so many uses.

X has its place in math. It is used for measurements as in 10' x 10'.

It can be used in sizing such as XL or 1X or 2X and so on.

You can use it to identify a spot where someone is to stand – X marks the spot.

X has also been used when someone is unable to sign their name, for whatever reason.

Then there's the famous X in XOXO signifying hugs and kisses to someone on text, in a card or a letter (remember those??).

X has also been used on maps to mark where a treasure just might be located.

If you are doing a presentation, X can indicate an amount you are unsure of, such as X number of dollars.

There are also uses for X in the alphabet of course but not so many especially, words that start with X as I mentioned before.

Regardless of religious beliefs, I have never liked the new version of the word "Christmas" as Xmas. It just seems wrong to me.

And where would we be without access to an x-ray machine when we need one.

As I started to think about the word "X", it was a little challenging but with a little research, I uncovered its true value and many uses. It's been an excellent addition to our vocabulary.

As always, I think about life and people. We all have value even if we don't see it at times. I had recently heard someone talk about a problem they weren't able to easily identify. They said it was like a pebble in their shoe. You can feel it. It's irritating. Ads yet, you just can't put your finger on it.

Sometimes, life is like that but, harder than a pebble to figure out. If we could only create an x-ray machine for emotions. Now that would be an excellent addition to our lives. Find the emotion and heal it.

The more I think about that. The more I like it. Some people are more in touch with their emotions than others so this super-duper x-ray machine could help those people help themselves. All in all, it's just another idea to help live our lives with maybe a little more happiness and satisfaction.

In the meantime, I guess we will just have to settle for X's many uses for the time being. There are many creative minds out there; maybe that new x-ray machine is coming one of these days.

YESTERDAY

Y is for Yesterday

We crucify ourselves between two thieves; regret for yesterday and fear of tomorrow. - Fulton Oursler

Yesterday: The day preceding this day; time in the immediate past; a short time ago.

Yesterday seems so long ago. Every day seems like the one before since we started with Covid.

I have had my moments when "why bother" creeps in and I seem to be fighting tiredness more often – of course that can't possibly be because I'm getting older. I like to think it's because of Covid Compromised Creativity. Many of us are suffering from my new made-up phrase because of the lack of interaction of yesterday.

I was saying to my BFF that it's been a year since I was in a clothing store. If you know me, you would know that I was kind of a clothes horse. I loooovvve my tops and my necklaces. Always have. I have easily survived not being in a store for a year. It's the connections of yesterday that are missing that I feel create a greater loss.

I think about yesterdays, before the border closed. I miss shopping trips to Grand Forks and Fargo, North Dakota but, it's not about the clothes. It's about the talks, the laughter and sharing with our friends. Oh and of course, the wine, it's always about enjoying the wine! I think about what will come of all of this **when, not if**, it's over. I know we have to find some meaning despite it all.

There are people that I speak to less often than before. I know most of us have more time on our hands but the communication has lessened or completely ended. Is there nothing to say? If that's it, that seems like such a tragedy.

Maybe it's time we stop talking about "yesterday" and talk about today. One day we will be out of this and then what? Will **caring** be the victim in all of this? I pray that's not the case.

We always look back. We think about the past. We remember the good and the bad. The important thing is to stop having the regret and bad feelings that come along with going backwards. It's so over. You can make peace in your heart by forgiving yourself and changing the focus to today.

We have all made mistakes. This has been a tough year. Let's make it a vow to stop beating ourselves up in the next one. Not one of us is perfect. Sorry, but that's the truth, so why do we keep expecting ourselves to be? We can so easily forgive others for their mistakes but when we look to our past, why is it so darn hard to forgive ourselves. Let's try and do that now so we can start fresh either tomorrow or the next day, if not today. I'm cheering for you.

So, as you look in the rear-view mirror, what do you see? The view forward is much larger than the view from the small mirror that looks behind. Perhaps it's time we took a lesson from that. Our lives might be on pause for a reason. We need to support each other through this and come out stronger on the other end. We also need to be stronger for ourselves. Let's do both. You in?

ZOOM

Z is for Zoom

"In A COVID-19 World, Don't Zoom Away Your Credibility.
Your attire and grooming are some of the simplest things
you can do to maintain your professional bearing."
Cindy Ann Peterson

Zoom: The act or process of zooming.

Does anyone remember the car commercial that went "zoom zoom zoom"? There's a young boy standing alone on a long, open stretch of highway and he turns around and says zoom zoom zoom into a camera and a car goes whipping by. It may have started with Mazda.

Where I'm going here is, I love words. I guess that's why I write. Our words change and vary over time. Some even get included in the dictionary. Like – why don't you "*google*" that?

Zoom is a word that has been around for a while but these days it has taken on an entirely new meaning. Zoom is how many people communicate. I have watched a zoom presentation with a room full of screens. The presenter is talking to people all over the world and their faces appear on the screens in front of the presenter. You can speak to them one on one. It's absolutely mind-boggling.

    Zoom rooms have become pretty common these days with the lockdown. You can have intimate groups with Zoom. You can record a class training on Zoom. There's even a free version. You can use a headset or not.

    I have even read with my great-nephew on Zoom. It's so much better than Facetime. My niece says, one of the rare times it's quiet in the house is, when we are reading together. It's not as good as a hug and being in the same room but it's certainly better than not seeing your favourite people, so I'll take it.

    I have used zoom to take classes, to chat one on one or participate as an onlooker in a presentation. All without having to leave home. I don't think that's a bad deal so thank you Zoom.

    So, zoom zoom zoom. Don't stay secluded. It's pretty simple, technology-wise, and it brings people into your homes in one of the few ways we can these days. If you're feeling a little lonely, reach out and zoom, zoom, zoom. You'll be glad you did.

About the Authors

The words in this book are a result of a collaboration between the authors. Many conversations, ideas, life experiences were discussed in hours upon hours of communication. Location didn't matter. It included chats on the phone, in cars, buses, boats, trains and planes, attending workshops, a book launch in Toronto with Jack Canfield and in Winnipeg at McNally. Sometimes, just a glass or two of wine on weekend getaways or at our favourite restaurant, our home away from home, "Bellamy's" in Winnipeg was all we needed to get the ideas going. It seems we never run out of things to talk about. Although we are very different people, we find common ground being united in wanting people that want more joy and peace in their lives to find a way to have it.

To order more books or have one delivered to someone that might enjoy this book, go to:

www.Amazon.ca
or
www.Amazon.com